GOD LOVES DOCTRINE

Moreno Dal Bello

"DOCTRINE!" It is one of the most despised words among many who consider themselves Christians. It is hated because it is considered to be that which divides Christians, causes strife and prevents unity among the brethren. "Doctrine divides," they say. "We need unity. We need to forget doctrine and all it's divisive qualities and concentrate on our mutual love for God. After all, it doesn't matter what you believe, but who you believe. We are all mere men and subject to error. We are all wrong in some area of doctrine but we are all sincere in our love for God, so let us put doctrine aside and allow our love for God, and His love for us, unite us and cause us to be as one." This all sounds so nice and is readily accepted as the Christian thing to do, and that it pleases God so much to see people casting aside their differences, respecting each other's point of view and endeavouring to live in ecumenical bliss.

A study of Scripture, however, will reveal that this is not the stand that God takes concerning doctrine. Doctrine, which means teaching, is a wonderful thing, if it is God's doctrine. The doctrine of Jesus Christ the Lord is given to men in order that they might know the True Christ, the True God and what He has said and what He wants His people to know, learn and love with all their hearts. Doctrine DOES divide; it does separate. It divides God's children from the children of wrath; it separates God's sheep from the cursed goats and it differentiates between

God's wheat and the Devil's tares. It is by doctrine that one can know God—Who He is and what He has done. It is through doctrine that God reveals Himself.

The word 'doctrine' is mentioned 51 times in the Bible: 6 times in the Old Testament and 45 times in the New Testament. The word 'doctrines' appears 5 times, all in the New Testament. The word 'doctrine' in the Old Testament can mean: something received, ie., mentally; instruction. Chastisement, reproof, warning; chastening, check, correction, discipline, rebuke. Something heard, an announcement, report, tidings. In The New Testament the word 'doctrine' can mean: Instruction (the act or the matter). Learning, teaching. Something said, communication, preaching, reason. So we see from a brief study of the meaning of the word 'doctrine', that the Christian has nothing to fear from it, no reason to stand aloof from it and absolutely no reason to despise it. It is a word and a thing that God loves. God's doctrine, His Word, His teachings, His Gospel, are all synonymous and anyone who claims to be a Christian and does not love God's Word, His teachings, His doctrine and His glorious Gospel are, at this moment, severely deluded. God has chosen to communicate His Gospel message by means of preaching, the preaching of doctrine by which He defines and distinguishes His Message from all others: "But hath in due times manifested His Word through preaching..." (Titus

1:3). "For after that in the wisdom of God the world by wisdom knew not God, it pleased God by the foolishness of preaching to save them that believe" (1 Cor.1:21).

The Bible has countless warnings of those who would come bringing false doctrine, unsound teaching, which deceives and leads men astray. It is vital that we pay strict attention to doctrine. We must be sure that the doctrine we hold to and abide in is truly the doctrine of Christ, lest we be found to be without God and without His Son (2 Jn.9-11).

Let us look now at some of the many instances where the word 'doctrine' is used in the Bible and see from God's very own Word that the doctrine of Christ is a good thing, a marvellous thing, a thing to be loved and cherished and a thing that every true believer abides in.

"Give ear, O ye heavens, and I will speak; and hear, O earth, the words of my mouth. My DOCTRINE shall drop as the rain, my speech shall distil as the dew, as the small rain upon the tender herb, and as the showers upon the grass" (Deut.32:1,2). This is the beginning of a song of Moses and in this preface he speaks of God's doctrine dropping as the rain. Rain is sent to make the earth fruitful. So, too, God's doctrine comes as refreshing rain to His people and makes the fruit of learning and knowledge to increase.

Solomon, in his Proverbs, writes: "Hear, ye children, the instruction of a father, and attend to know understanding. For I give you good DOCTRINE, forsake ye not my law" (Prov.4:1,2). There is good doctrine and there is bad doctrine. Doctrine which is true and doctrine which is false. Doctrine which comes from devils and the traditions of men and doctrine which comes from God. As we shall see later from Scripture, the Christian is to abide in good doctrine, in true doctrine. He is to be sure that he hears and speaks only that which is good doctrine and is to avoid those who speak bad doctrine, that doctrine which is not in accord with God's Doctrine. One has written, "We must look upon our teachers as our fathers, who love us and seek our welfare. We are told (v. 1), not only that it is the instruction of a father, but that it is understanding, and therefore should be welcome to intelligent creatures. Christianity has reason on its side, and we are taught it by fair reasoning. It is a law indeed (v.2), but that law is founded upon unquestionable principles of truth, upon GOOD DOCTRINE, which is worthy of all acceptation. If we admit the doctrine, we cannot but submit to the law."

"Whom shall he teach knowledge? And whom shall he make to understand doctrine? Them that are weaned from the milk, and drawn from the breasts" (Isa.28:9). The prophets and ministers of God are given to teach a knowledge of God and His Will in order to make His doctrine understood. This is how the Lord deals with His people. He teaches them by way of His holy doctrine. "They also that erred in spirit shall come to understanding, and they that murmured shall learn DOCTRINE" (Isa.29:24). Here we see that understanding and doctrine are intertwined. They cannot be separated. One cannot learn of God unless it is by doctrine. One can know of the existence of a Creator God by looking at a flower, but to learn of that God—to know Who He is and what He has done, to learn about His Son, Redemption, Salvation and Substitution—one must be taught the doctrine of God. One cannot have understanding unless one has been taught good doctrine by the Holy God. It is by revealed doctrine that we come to an understanding of Who God is and what He has done. It is after hearing the doctrine of the Gospel of Jesus Christ that a man believes and trusts in the True Christ: "That we should be to the praise of His glory, who first trusted in Christ. In Whom ye also trusted, AFTER that ye heard the Word of Truth, the GOSPEL of your salvation: in whom after that ye believed, ye were sealed with that Holy Spirit of promise" (Eph.1:12,13). The Gospel has been commanded, by the Lord Jesus Christ, to be preached to every creature (Mk.16:15). To preach is to teach and to teach is to indoctrinate, in the sense of imparting learning, or, to instruct.

That ends our brief look at the word 'doctrine' as found in the Old Testament. There are many more instances in the Old Testament where words such as 'instruction', 'teaching' or 'teacheth' are mentioned where the word 'doctrine' could just as easily have been used. In this age where most people's authority on the religious is through their subjective experiences, it will surprise most professing believers that the New Testament is where the majority of verses containing the word 'doctrine' are found. It is not merely an Old Testament word, but is very much a New Testament word prevalent on the lips of the Lord Jesus, as well as in the inspired writings of the apostles.

"And it came to pass, when Jesus had ended these sayings, the people were astonished at His DOCTRINE: for He taught them as one having authority, and not as the scribes" (Matt.7:28,29; see also Matt.22:33; Mk.1:22, 27; Lk.4:32; Acts 13:12). When the Lord Jesus spoke He taught doctrine. Whenever people sat at Jesus' feet they heard doctrine. The Lord Jesus loves to teach, He loves to teach and instruct His people. This is evident throughout the Gospels of Matthew, Mark, Luke and John and in the Book of Revelation. Jesus taught through doctrine and it is in this very doctrine, the doctrine of Christ, that every believer should and does abide (2 Jn.9). Those who hear Jesus' sayings and do according to His will, made known to us through His doctrine, are as those who build their houses upon the rock. Those who do not are as those who have built on sand, whose houses will not stand (Matt. 7:24-27).

The Bible warns that there is a doctrine which the believer is not to hear or to obey and that is false doctrine: "Cease, my son, to hear the instruction that causeth to err from the words of knowledge" (Prov.19:27). There is doctrine that causes strife and confusion. False doctrines are the teachings that come from man's imagination and not from God's Word. False doctrines are nothing but fables designed to deceive and delude, and the only way a man can be free from false doctrine is to be full of good doctrine—the doctrine which comes from God. "Then understood they how that He bade them not beware of the leaven of bread, but of the doctrine of the Pharisees and of the Sadducees" (Matt.16:12). The Lord Jesus warns us that not all doctrine we will hear, which comes to us in the name of Jesus, is good doctrine: "For many shall come in My name, saying, I am Christ; and shall deceive many" (Matt.24:5). False doctrine abounds in our day. It is believed by the majority of professing believers and is taught by their most revered and respected teachers. The Bible says that men will heap unto themselves teachers who would speak fables unto them and speak peace to them (2 Tim.4:3,4). False doctrine is spoken by false preachers, who themselves do not abide in the doctrine of Christ, but in the doctrines which come from their own minds. Churches today, both Protestant and others, are filled with false doctrine which comes like a flood from the pulpits of false teachers. The best protection against false doctrine is to be well armed with the true doctrine which comes from God. The Christian is to "Stand therefore, having your loins girt about with truth..." (Eph.6:14). The way we learn God's truth is through doctrine. The true believer who is born of God, is clothed with God's very Truth which is very much a necessary part of the Christian's armour, and abides in it eternally.

"And He taught them many things by parables, and said unto them in His DOCTRINE..." (Mk.4:2). Here we see further proof of the Lord Jesus teaching people by doctrine. How else can a man teach another unless it is done by instruction, by a series of teachings, or doctrines, in order to get his message across? Those who say they hate doctrine fail to realise that every time they hear a sermon they are hearing doctrine, whether good or bad. Everyone believes doctrine. Everyone who attends a church service or reads a book or listens to a taped message, is being fed some sort of doctrine. It is because of doctrine that they choose their particular denomination. What is taught about what the Bible says, is what attracts people to a particular church. Though the lives of many professing christians run on experience, it is certain doctrines by which they arrived at their present state. When they read their Bibles they read nothing but doctrine, the doctrine of God. In fact, the Bible could more properly be called 'THE DOCTRINES (ie., teachings) OF GOD'.

"And the scribes and chief priests heard it, and sought how they might destroy Him: for they feared Him, because all the people was astonished at His DOCTRINE" (Mk.11:18). Here we see religionists and their response to the God of the Universe and His doctrine. These religious leaders hated the Lord Jesus, for they hated His doctrine. They don't hate doctrine itself but they do hate the doctrine which comes from God. Listen to how the Lord Jesus addresses such people: "And the Father Himself, which hath sent Me, hath borne witness of Me. Ye have neither heard His voice at any time, nor seen His shape. And YE HAVE NOT HIS WORD ABIDING IN YOU: for Whom He hath sent, Him ye believe not" (Jn.5:37,38). The Bible is replete with doctrine which identifies and distinguishes the Person and Work of Jesus Christ. Those who reject this doctrine, who do not see the True Jesus in the witness God has borne of Him, do not have the Word of God abiding in them. They have the word of another. They hold to false doctrine and are yet in their sins. False religious leaders fear God and His Doctrine and would like nothing better than to destroy God and His Doctrine, to eradicate it from the face of the earth. Not to eradicate religion, or the notion of a Supreme Being, but to do away completely with God's absolute teachings. They hated Christ and His doctrine, so too, they hate, and will forever hate, Christ's people and the doctrine of Christ which they abide in and teach. Jesus warned by

His doctrine of those religious leaders who love to be seen by others as religious and who love positions of authority and respect but who are empty wagons when it comes to teaching the doctrines of Christ. They make a lot of noise but carry no truth. "And he said unto him in His DOCTRINE, Beware of the scribes, which love to go in long clothing, and love salutations in the market places...these shall receive greater damnation" (Mk.12:38,40).

"Jesus answered them, and said, My doctrine is not Mine, But His that sent Me" (Jn.7:16). The Lord Jesus brought to this earth not His own doctrine, that is, His doctrine was not that which He had learned of men, but it was given to Him by Divine Inspiration. Christ's doctrine is God's doctrine. Hebrews 1 tells us that God speaks to man in these last days by His glorious doctrine through His Divine Son: "(God) hath in these last days spoken unto us by His Son, Whom He hath appointed Heir of all things, by Whom also He made the worlds" (Heb.1:2).

The high priest, Caiaphas, desired to prove Christ a false prophet, a false preacher, and he endeavoured to do this by exposing His doctrine: "The high priest then asked Jesus of His disciples, and of His doctrine" (Jn.18:19). To prove one a false preacher, one is not to judge according to outward appearance, nor even of reputation. A man is judged by His doctrine. Whom does he say Christ is? What does He teach that Christ has done? Even the high priest knew this. Jesus Christ encouraged his enemies to test His doctrine to see whether it came from God: "If any man will do His will, he shall know of the doctrine, whether it be of God, or whether I speak of Myself" (Jn.7:17). Every child of God believes and teaches Christ's doctrine. Those who are not of God hold to false doctrine and these are they which we are to avoid insofar as fellowship is concerned (2 Jn.9-11). Doctrine is that whereby we can discern whether a man knows God and His Gospel or not. Paul the apostle warned of those who would come preaching false doctrine, which amounted to another gospel wherein is no salvation. He said of those men that they were in an accursed state. He did not say they were Christians who were in error, but that they were people under the wrath of God (Gal.1:8,9), for if the Gospel be hid it is hid to them that are lost, not merely in error (2 Cor.4:3). Paul taught that the way the Galatians would know whether a man was in an accursed state or saved was if they came preaching the right doctrine: the Gospel of Christ which Paul had preached to them. If they preached the wrong gospel, then regardless of how moral and upright they were in the sight of men it proved they were, up to that point in time, in a lost state being ignorant of the doctrine of Christ (Rom.10:1-4).

    The Bible shows that God's children abide in His doctrine, for they love Him and His teachings: "And they continued steadfastly in the apostle's DOCTRINE and fellowship, and in breaking of bread, and in prayers" (Acts 2:42). One cannot have union and fellowship, two cannot walk together the Bible says, unless they be agreed (Amos 3:3). And two cannot have true Christian union and fellowship unless they are agreed as to the doctrine of Christ: Who He is and what He has done. Acts 2:42 shows that the believers sat together and fellowshipped in harmony for they all believed in the same doctrine. They were of one mind for they all had the mind of Christ (1 Cor.2:16). Of course, these believers along with believers today, did not agree about everything but they did agree about the Person and Work of Christ Jesus and how a man is saved, for they had all been taught of God (Jn.6:45). Christians throughout the centuries have heard the same doctrines, which taught the same Gospel, which tells of the same Christ Who came to redeem His own (Titus 2:14). True Christian fellowship does not come by compromising doctrine and casting aside truth for the sake of 'love', but in believing in and continuing in the doctrine of Christ. Unity at the cost of truth is satanic!! Those in the Book of Acts ate together and they all rejoiced as one, for they all had one mind when it came to doctrine. They adhered to, believed in and continued in the doctrine of the apostles which they had received directly from Christ Himself. The doctrine of Christ is the core element in proper Christian unity and fellowship.

The enemies of the cross have a deep and lasting hatred for Christ's doctrine. "...Did not we straitly command you that ye should not TEACH in this name? and, behold, ye have filled Jerusalem with your DOCTRINE, and intend to bring this man's blood upon us" (Acts 5:28). The apostles were not told to cease performing miracles of healings and casting out demons but were vehemently warned against teaching doctrine in Christ's name. Again, the attack and attention of God's enemies was against God's doctrine. It is upon God's doctrine that Satan focuses his acutest attention and plans his most intense and subtle attacks. Millions who believed they were Christians and called Jesus Christ, "LORD", will discover to their amazement on that Judgement Day that they were never Christians for Christ did not know them (Matt.7:21-23): millions of deluded people in hell for all eternity, who were deceived by the subtle false doctrines of Satan and his ministers, all of whom are transformed as the ministers of righteousness (2 Cor.11:14,15; Rom.16:17,18). It was this 'new' doctrine which Jesus the Christ taught that the religious leaders in Acts knew was leading away their followers and they were desperate to put an end to the preaching of it. God's enemies today hate God's doctrine no less than the religious leaders did in the Book of Acts. They rubbish doctrine; they put it down. They mock those who preach it and who place great emphasis on doctrine. They don't want to hear it. They don't want to know it. One man told me 'I'm not interested in your doctrine'. What he was really saying was that he was not interested in the doctrine of Christ Jesus the Lord of which I was informing him. He has his own beliefs and holds to the teachings he has heard and likes, and is not interested in God's Truth. People such as this man are referred to in 2 Thessalonians 2:10-12: "And with all deceivableness of unrighteousness in them that perish; because THEY RECEIVED NOT THE LOVE OF THE TRUTH, that they might be saved. And for this cause God shall send them strong delusion, that they should believe a lie: that they all might be damned who believed not the truth, but had pleasure in unrighteousness." They only want their own 'deep heart experiences' with God. They live in a world of the mystical and have no time for the objective hard truth which comes to us from God in the form of doctrine. False religious leaders are averse to sound doctrine and are murderers of men's souls.

    In order to learn about the God whom the apostle Paul spoke of, the Athenians asked Paul "...may we know what this new DOCTRINE, whereof thou speakest, is?" (Acts 17:19). The apostle then proceeded to teach, to instruct the Athenians, by way of doctrine as to Who God is and what He had done, including teaching the doctrine of repentance toward God and the Resurrection of His Son Jesus Christ. Paul did not mention the many miracles he had done or even those which Jesus Himself had done, but he taught doctrine which told of the Person of God and the Works of God. Paul did not flood the Athenians with a wave of subjective experiences and how wonderful God can make you feel or how moral one can become by following this God etc. No, Paul told about God: His Person and His works and of His Son, that they might know by this 'new doctrine' who the real God is and what the real God had done. God Himself has taught in His Word what He is like and, by this, has distinguished Himself from all false gods: "Remember the former things of old: for I am God, and there is none else; I am God, and there is none like Me, declaring the end from the beginning, and from ancient times the things that are not yet done, saying, My Counsel shall stand, and I will do all My pleasure: calling a ravenous bird from the east, the man that executeth My counsel from a far country: yea, I have spoken it, I will also bring it to pass; I have purposed it, I will also do it" (Isa.46:9-11).

    The apostle Paul, in writing to the Christians at Rome, rejoiced that they, though once servants of sin and children of wrath, had now been converted. This was evidenced, not principally by their moral reformations, but by their abiding in God's glorious doctrine: "But God be thanked, that ye were the servants of sin, but ye have obeyed from the heart that form of DOCTRINE which was delivered you" (Rom.6:17). This verse teaches that the true believers spoken about here had obeyed from the heart, that form (meaning a die or stamp) of doctrine. "The metaphor is that of a cast or frame into which molten material is poured so as to take its shape." This doctrine to which the Roman believers had become obedient, is the very same doctrine, God's Gospel, which Paul had preached elsewhere. Paul did not speak here of their moral reformations but of their obedience to the doctrine which came from God, which defined His great Gospel. Many say that "Not all are theologians" and that "one does not need to know doctrine, they just have to know Him." But the only way a person CAN know God is by the very doctrine of Christ which identifies His Person and Work and distinguishes Him from all counterfeits. People say it is not important WHAT you believe but WHOM you believe! But surely WHAT you believe about whom you believe DEFINES the one you believe! After all, it is a man's doctrine which identifies and distinguishes the god he worships and serves. The True Christ is revealed in the Bible, which is the Word (doctrines, ie. teachings) of God (see Rom.10:14,15), and no one is saved by hearing and believing false doctrine. Salvation itself is incompatible with ignorance of the doctrine which teaches Who Christ is and what Christ has done.

Doctrine is so essential, so vital, and so central to the Christian life that Paul warns in these next verses that any who came preaching any other doctrine apart from that doctrine which they had received from him, were to be avoided: "Now I beseech you, brethren, MARK THEM WHICH CAUSE DIVISIONS AND OFFENCES CONTRARY TO THE DOCTRINE WHICH YE HAVE LEARNED; and AVOID THEM. For THEY THAT ARE SUCH SERVE NOT OUR LORD JESUS CHRIST, but their own belly; and BY GOOD WORDS AND FAIR SPEECHES DECEIVE the hearts of the simple" (Rom.16:17,18). Notice here that it was not Paul the apostle or any other who brought sound doctrine who were causing division, but those who came with UNSOUND teachings were the ones who caused the division and offences! Good doctrine is not the enemy of the Church; it is bad doctrine, false doctrine which is our enemy! It is not good doctrine which deceives but false doctrine. If one speaks and teaches the sound doctrine of God then one is obeying the Lord and doing His work (1 Tim.4:6). Those who come opposing God's doctrine in any way are called enemies of the cross (Phil.3:18,19) and should be avoided for they speak not according to wisdom but according to their own deceitful hearts. They are the ones who serve not the Lord Jesus Christ. They are deceivers who serve only themselves, troublemakers who are opposed to the sound words of good doctrine.

The Christian is taught to beware of false doctrine many times in Scripture. It is the only form of doctrine that the believer is to have nothing to do with. "That we henceforth be no more children, tossed to and fro, and carried about with every wind of doctrine, by the sleight of men, and cunning craftiness, whereby they lie in wait to deceive" (Eph.4:14). The Devil and his ministers are so very subtle. They deceive the hearts of the simple with many and varied doctrines which take away from the finished work of Christ or add to what He has done. Those who do not know the Truth are blown about with the many false doctrines which abound in our day and which come under the guise of 'salvation by grace'. Those who are fixed in God's Word, who are grounded in God's Truth and who abide in the doctrine of Christ, cannot and will not be moved from His glorious Truth (Jn.6:68).

Paul continues his warnings against false doctrine in this next Scripture and emphasizes that it is only Christ's doctrine that we are to teach and believe: "As I besought thee to abide still at Ephesus, when I went into Macedonia, that thou mightest charge some that they teach no other doctrine" (1 Tim.1:3). Doctrine is so important and we need to believe accurately God's Gospel– His testimony of Who Christ is, what Christ has done and for whom He has done it. No other doctrine should be believed or taught as Christ's doctrine other than what God teaches in His Holy

Word. No straying from His doctrine is permitted, for anything added to or taken away from God's doctrine turns the Gospel into another gospel, which is no gospel at all for it tells of a false christ. Christians believe God's doctrine and no other. Christians teach God's doctrine and no other AND SHOULD NOT SIT UNDER THE TEACHING OF A FALSE MINISTER PREACHING FALSE DOCTRINE for this will not profit at all: "Cease, my son, to hear the instruction that causeth to err from the words of knowledge" (Prov.19:27; see also Gal.5:7-9 & 2 Jn.4).

The Church of God, which is the believers who make up the Body of Christ, should not 'be' the pillar of truth, IT IS THE PILLAR OF TRUTH!! "But if I tarry long, that thou mayest know how thou oughtest to behave thyself in the house of God, which IS the church of the living God, the pillar and the ground of the truth" (1 Tim.3:15).

Paul instructed Timothy in this next passage that the law was not made for a righteous man but for sinful men, which includes, "...whoremongers, for them that defile themselves with mankind, for menstealers, for liars, for perjured persons, and if there be any other thing that is contrary to SOUND DOCTRINE." What is the sound doctrine that is here spoken of? The very next verse tells us: "According to the glorious GOSPEL of the blessed God, which was committed to my trust" (1 Tim.1:10,11). The Christian is to avoid, to have no part with, those who teach or do anything which is contrary to sound doctrine which is the Gospel of Christ, the Word of Truth (Eph.1:13). "Be ye not unequally yoked together with unbelievers: for what fellowship hath righteousness with unrighteousness? And what communion hath light with darkness?" (2 Cor.6:14).

    Paul continues his instruction to Timothy in this next verse: "If thou put the brethren in remembrance of these things, thou shalt be a good minister of Jesus Christ, nourished up in the words of faith and of GOOD DOCTRINE, whereunto thou hast attained" (1 Tim.4:6). There was a man this writer knew who resisted doctrine and encouraged me to just "go to God's word and don't look for doctrine." He advised me to simply allow myself 'to be nourished by God's Word'. Well, this Scripture shows clearly that the Christian is indeed to be nourished up in the words of faith AND also of good DOCTRINE! It is good doctrine, which may also be described as words of faith, that nourishes the believer. The world and religion simply hate Christ's doctrine. They see absolutes and dogmatic teaching as something evil, but we see that the Bible is full of absolutes and dogmatic teaching. It is a good and proper thing to be very dogmatic when it comes to the doctrine of Christ. For instance, it teaches that there is only ONE Way to the Father and that is through His Son Jesus Christ the Lord and so forth. The Bible teaches that good spiritual nourishment comes from the words of faith and from good doctrine and these things are to be found only in Holy Scripture, the Word of God.

Again, in this next verse Paul the apostle emphasizes the significance of doctrine in the life of the believer: "Till I come, give attendance to reading, to exhortation, TO DOCTRINE" and later Paul says "take heed unto thyself, and unto the DOCTRINE; continue in them: for in doing this thou shalt both save thyself, and them that hear thee" (1 Tim.4:13,16). The Christian is to give attendance, he is to pay attention to and allow himself to be instructed by God's good doctrine. He is to take heed unto the doctrine of God and be ruled by the teachings of Christ as found in Scripture, particularly the doctrine which teaches that man, in and of himself, cannot come to God for he is without God and therefore without hope in this world and must be drawn by the Father to the Son purely by grace alone. That man is dead in sin and cannot come to God in and of himself is a root doctrine of salvation by grace alone. The doctrine/Gospel of Christ teaches that man is saved purely by grace through faith and that this faith is not of ourselves it is the gift of God (Eph.2:8,9). Man is not to be blown about by his many and varied feelings about what is 'right' and 'of God', but he is to be taught by, and must abide in, the doctrine of Christ as found in Holy Scripture.

Those who teach doctrine are worthy of great honor: "Let the elders that rule well be counted worthy of double honor, especially they who labor in the word and DOCTRINE" (1 Tim.5:17). Those who teach and abide in Christ's doctrine should be listened to, for the Lord God has appointed men to be teachers of His very Gospel, the only Gospel that saves. Praise God for the many wonderful men He has appointed to the Church, to teach with clarity and simplicity the glorious Gospel of God wherein the Righteousness of Christ is revealed (Rom.1:16,17).

Perhaps the apostle Paul spoke no clearer, when dealing with true doctrine and those who taught otherwise, than in this next passage. Hear, and hear well, the words which Almighty God inspired Paul to write: "If any man teach otherwise, and consent not to wholesome words, even the words of our Lord Jesus Christ, and to the DOCTRINE which is according to godliness; he is proud, KNOWING NOTHING, but doting about questions and strifes of words, whereof cometh envy, strife, railings, evil surmisings, perverse disputings of men of corrupt minds, and DESTITUTE OF THE TRUTH, supposing that gain is godliness: FROM SUCH WITHDRAW THYSELF" (1 Tim.6:3-5). Here we see clearly that those men who set themselves up as Christian ministers and pastors, yet who come teaching doctrine which is contrary to what the apostle Paul taught and are not conformed to wholesome words, the doctrine of Christ which is according to godliness, are proud men who know nothing and who cause trouble and strife. These false teachers are, the Bible says, destitute of the truth. Isaiah 8:20 says of these men: To the law and to the testimony: if they speak not according to this word, it is because THERE IS NO LIGHT IN THEM." The Bible does not teach that there is some light in these men or that they speak some truth, it says clearly that there is NO light in them for they are destitute of God's Truth, even though they come in His name and proclaim that Jesus is Lord! These men are the ones every true believer should withdraw himself from and have nothing further to do with. The Christian has no business whatsoever attending a church service where a false gospel is taught by men who have no light and know not and abide not in the doctrine of Christ. The Bible says that they have not God (2 Jn.9).

The following verse speaks for itself: "All Scripture is given by inspiration of God, and is profitable for DOCTRINE, for reproof, for correction, for instruction in righteousness" (2 Tim.3:16). The primary thing which all Scripture is profitable for is DOCTRINE. Teaching is what God does and teaching is what the Bible is full of. It is God's Book of instruction for every one who will believe.

Another solemn warning is given by the apostle Paul in this following passage: "Preach the Word; be instant in season, out of season;

reprove, rebuke, exhort with all longsuffering and DOCTRINE. For the time will come when they will not endure SOUND doctrine; but after their own lusts shall they heap to themselves teachers, having itching ears; And they shall turn away their ears from the truth, and shall be turned unto fables" (2 Tim.4:2-4). If you are not being taught sound doctrine, then you are listening to fables which have not lead you to the True Christ. The Christian is to preach the word of God and to instruct with patience and doctrine. How else can a man be instructed lest he be taught? And how can he be taught unless it is by way of doctrine? And how can he, in turn, teach unless it is by doctrine, the same doctrine which he has heard? Paul warns of the time that would come, indeed which is now arrived, when men would not endure sound doctrine but would attend to those who speak fables and lies who have not the truth of God. These are the men and these are the sorts of teachings, doctrines, which men follow by nature. False teachings and unsound doctrine is all that is left when one turns away his ears from God's Truth. So many today follow the religion of subjective experience. Feelings and false doctrine are the core elements in the religion of today and most have ears only for the lies of men and not for the Word, the doctrines of God. What most people today believe is Christianity, is nothing more than a delusion. There is nothing Christian about it!

Paul wrote to Titus that it was to be by sound doctrine whereby he could both exhort and convince those who spoke against the Truth: "Holding fast the faithful word as he hath been taught, that he may be able by sound DOCTRINE both to exhort and convince the gainsayers" (Titus 1:9). This verse is part of the qualifications Paul gave of those who would be bishops. The word for bishop in the New Testament is overseer. Again, this verse shows us the importance and relevance of doctrine if we are to properly present the Gospel of God. "But speak thou the things which become sound doctrine" (Titus 2:1). Here Paul is saying that Titus should speak sound doctrine only. More evidence is presented here that it is sound doctrine which the Christian must teach and continue to hear and learn and understand, for it is through God's revelation of His doctrines that we know Him and understand Him more and more and increase in our knowledge of Who God is and what His great Gospel is all about. "And this is life eternal, that they might KNOW THEE the only true God, and Jesus Christ, Whom Thou hast sent" (Jn.17:3).

Paul teaches in this next passage that Titus should teach the young men to speak God's doctrine with exactness and preciseness, at the same time showing that it is most surely possible to do this: "In all things shewing thyself a pattern of good works; in doctrine shewing uncorruptness, gravity, sincerity" (Titus 2:7). If Titus was to teach

God's doctrine with uncorruptness, then it is of a surety that Paul taught it thus and therefore we are to believe it with equal accuracy and also teach it with uncorruptness. The teaching of God's doctrines is to be accompanied with gravity and sincerity and not with humor as is most popular today among those who come in Christ's name but teach not the doctrine of Christ. To be a true Christian is to know and abide in Christ's doctrine. We are to know what it is that God teaches in His Word. We are to know without a shadow of a doubt what it is that God has done by sending His glorious and only Begotten Son into this world before we can believe it, and we are to teach and to preach His doctrine, the glorious Gospel, to every creature. We do not get saved by our knowledge of doctrine but our knowledge of and abidance in the doctrine of Christ is the evidence that we know Him and are most surely saved. God teaches His sheep and Christ has said that: "My sheep hear My voice, and I know them, and they follow Me" (Jn.10:27). And, "...Everyone that is of the Truth heareth My voice" (Jn.18:37), that is they hear and understand and receive Christ's teachings: His Testimony of Who He is and what He has done.

      Perhaps the clearest Scripture in the whole Bible in regards to the importance, the prominence and the absolute necessity of knowing God's doctrine is this next verse: "Whosoever transgresseth and ABIDETH NOT IN THE

DOCTRINE OF CHRIST, HATH NOT GOD. He that abideth in the doctrine of Christ, he hath both the Father and the Son" (2 Jn.9). Again, knowledge of God's doctrine is not a condition for salvation, it is an evidence that one has truly been taught of God and been born again (Jn.6:45). This verse shows clearly that every true Christian does truly abide in the doctrine of Christ which is His Holy Gospel message, that salvation is by grace alone through faith alone in Christ's obedience and death. It also shows that everyone who does not know and abide in Christ's doctrine IS NOT A CHRISTIAN. It proves that Christ's doctrine can be known, indeed is known, by all who are His children who have had their sins imputed to Christ and His glorious Righteousness imputed unto them. Those who oppose Christ's doctrine, His Gospel, have not God neither have they the Son and are in a lost state. The Bible says, "But if our Gospel be hid, it is hid to them that are LOST" (2 Cor.4:3). Ignorance of the Gospel is evidence of lostness. Ignorance of doctrine is no excuse, for if the blind follow the blind both shall fall into the ditch (Matt.15:14). Ignorance is the refuge of the damned. Those who are ignorant of the Righteousness of Christ go about trying to establish a righteousness of their own in hope of one day being saved and accepted by God. They show that they are in a damned state–dead to God and alive to sin. Look what Paul said about the Jews of his day: "For they being ignorant of God's Righteousness, and going about to establish their own righteousness, have not submitted themselves unto the Righteousness of God" (Rom.10:3). "But Israel, which followed after the law of righteousness, hath not attained to the law of righteousness. Wherefore? Because they sought it not by faith, but as it were by the works of the law. For they stumbled at that stumblingstone" (Rom.9:31,32). That stumbling stone is the Righteousness of Jesus Christ which is the only ground of salvation.

     In this next verse the apostle John teaches what Paul so often emphasized, that the Christian should have no part with those who oppose God's doctrine and who hear not the voice of Him who seeks and delivers His sheep: If there come any unto you, and bring not THIS doctrine, receive him not into your house, neither bid him God speed for he that biddeth him God speed is PARTAKER OF HIS EVIL DEEDS" (2 Jn.10,11). Those who heard John were familiar with the doctrine he preached and taught. They believed in Christ's one and only Gospel and knew without a shadow of a doubt when one came to them preaching any other doctrine than the one they had heard and believed. The true believer is to have no religious fellowship with those who abide not in the doctrine of Christ, regardless of how much the person may claim to love Christ and say he is Lord etc. False christians are just as dangerous and should be just as much avoided as false doctrine. They should be told true doctrine, the doctrine of Christ but should they reject it and close the door to the Gospel, we then should have no fellowship with them until they come to believe the doctrine of God which teaches the Gospel of Christ Jesus the Lord.

The Lord Jesus Christ literally hates false doctrine. False doctrine is repulsive to a Holy God and is so to all His people. To slander a man is a very serious crime. How much more serious an offence is it when man slanders the God of the Universe by preaching false doctrine which promotes lies about the True Character of God and what He has done. The people of God hear only the Good Shepherd's voice and not that of a stranger (Jn.10:4,5). See here what the Lord Jesus Himself says about false doctrine: "So hast thou also them that hold the doctrine of the Nicolaitans, WHICH THING I HATE" (Rev.2:15). Any doctrine which does not speak of God's only Gospel, which alone presents God's only Jesus, is a hated thing by God Himself. There is no salvation to be found in false doctrine. It is right and proper for the Christian to hate all false doctrine for it speaks lies about God's Gospel and distorts the truth about the Person and Work of the Lord Jesus Christ. The Lord Jesus commended the Christians at Ephesus who tested those who claimed to be apostles and were not, and found them to be liars, false preachers of false doctrine (Rev.2:2).

Jesus Christ often warned of those who taught lies yet presented them as the very doctrines of God: "But in vain do they worship Me, teaching for doctrines the commandments of men" (Matt.15:9; see also Mk.7:7). He described false teachers as wolves in sheeps clothing (Matt.7:15). False teachers come with false doctrines, teaching them as the very doctrines of Christ, yet they speak lies and the only way to know that they speak lies is if one has the truth. The only way I know that $2 + 2 = 5$ is wrong is because I know that the true answer is 4. If one is truly born again, born of God, then one will have the doctrines of Christ and will forever reject and withdraw himself from all other doctrines.

Warnings of false doctrines are again made clear by Paul the apostle in this next verse of Scripture: "Now the Spirit speaketh expressly, that in the latter times some shall depart from the faith, giving heed to seducing spirits, and doctrines of devils" (1 Tim.4:1). Here Paul teaches that the Holy Spirit explicitly teaches that in the latter times, in which we now are, some would turn away from the truth, from Christ's doctrine, and take heed to the doctrines of devils. This would show that these people were never true believers for had they been, "...they would NO DOUBT have continued with us: but they went out, that they might be made manifest that they were not all of us" (1 Jn.2:19). Now you should be able to see more clearly than ever that if you do not abide in the doctrine of Christ you abide in the doctrine of devils and have not God, for no child of God abides in false doctrine, the doctrine which comes from devils. NO ONE WAS EVER SAVED BY BELIEVING IN FALSE DOCTRINE, for how can a person believing in false doctrine, which amounts to a false gospel which tells of another christ, abide in the doctrine of Christ?

The writer of Hebrews teaches clearly that Jesus Christ does not change. That is, who He is and what He has done does not change with time but remains the same forever. "Jesus Christ the same yesterday, and today, and for ever. (Therefore) be not carried about with divers and STRANGE DOCTRINES, for it is a good thing that the heart be established with grace; not with meats, which have not profited them that have been occupied therein" (Heb.13:8,9; see also Mal.3:6). Do not be moved by new and strange doctrines which Christ and the apostles did not teach. Christians today are like Christians were in the Book of Acts: they continue steadfastly in the apostle's doctrine (Acts 2:42). Who Jesus Christ is and what Jesus Christ has done, has not and will not ever change. He is the Son of God who came to this earth to live a life of perfect obedience to God and to die on the accursed tree for the sins of His people, whom He came to save. The doctrine of Christ which was taught and believed in the apostle's day is the same doctrine which is taught and believed by every true believer today. Do not be moved by new doctrines, so-called new revelations about Jesus. Believe the old, old

Gospel which is no less than God's Testimony of the Person and Work of Christ for His elect.

    Jesus Christ was sent by God the Father to this earth to save His people from their sins (Gal.4:4,5 & Lk.1:77). A people who were dead in their sins and dead to God: "And you hath He quickened, who were dead in trespasses and sins" (Eph.2:1). A people who could not and would not come to God, God's Way (Rom.3:10-12). A people who went about according to their fallen nature, doing what was right in their eyes, trying to establish a righteousness of their own in the hope of pleasing a Just and Holy God. Jesus Christ came to this earth to save all those whom the Father had given Him: "As Thou hast given Him power over all flesh, that He should give eternal life to as many as Thou hast given Him" (Jn.17:2; see also Jn.17:6,8,9,14-20). These are they whom God has chosen from before the foundation of the world: "According as He hath chosen us in Him before the foundation of the world..." (Eph.1:4). Jesus Christ came to this earth to live a life of perfect obedience and to bear, or carry away, the sins of His people, which were imputed unto Him, or charged to His account, and Whose Righteousness was imputed unto them: "For He hath made Him to be sin for us, who knew no sin; that we might be made the Righteousness of God in Him" (2 Cor.5:21). Jesus Christ came to this earth to fulfill the Father's will by saving all whom the Father had elected from before the foundation of the world. All Christ's sheep will hear and obey His voice and follow Him and they will never perish, but be preserved in Christ eternally: "My sheep hear My voice, and I know them, and they follow Me: and I give unto them eternal life; and they shall never perish, neither shall any man pluck them out of My hand" (Jn.10:27,28). All His people will repent of their every sin and turn forever from ever having believed that they could do anything to satisfy God's Justice and be obedient enough to merit God's favor (2 Tim.2:25). The apostle Paul said of all his religion and all that he had done and believed in before hearing and abiding in the doctrine of Christ: "Yea doubtless, and I count all things but loss for the excellency of the knowledge of Christ Jesus my Lord: for whom I have suffered the loss of all things, and do count them but dung, that I may win Christ, and be found in Him not having mine own righteousness, which is of the law, but that which is through the faith of Christ, the righteousness which is of God by faith" (Phil.3:8,9).

This is the Jesus that every Christian believes in. This is the doctrine of Christ which every true believer abides in. Those who claim to be believers and those who claim to have been born again whilst ignorant of Christ's doctrine, have not God and are yet in their sins (Rom.10:1-4). Many cannot part with the years of religion and church attendance they were a part of before hearing God's only Gospel wherein Christ's Righteousness is revealed (Rom. 1:16,17). This is like saying that one arrived at one's destination before they got there! It simply cannot be done. Many refuse to accept, and therefore repent of, the fact that their religious works and beliefs prior to hearing and believing in God's only Gospel were dead works and idolatry. Such a person is lost at this point in time because they are basing their salvation on something other than God's Gospel. Belief of the Truth is a distinguishing feature of every true believer (2Thess.2:13,14). Professing believers, that is, those who claim to have been saved prior to hearing and believing in God's Gospel, have redefined God's Gospel by trusting in some mystical experience which has convicted them of God's existence or of the historical fact that Jesus Christ died on a cross, or on the strength of some moral reformation which even atheists can experience. Millions of lost people today believe that God existed and that Christ died on a cross for sins. People of every religion experience great changes in their lives, but none except the elect of God ever see and believe in God's Gospel which reveals the highly significant fact that Christ died according to the Scriptures (1 Cor.15:1-3). Paul the apostle had years of religious duty and moral uprightness which he thought recommended himself to God. Imagine how many times Paul had been under the impression that God was answering his many prayers. But on learning of Christ and His Righteousness, as revealed in God's glorious Gospel, Paul turned his back on and repented of all his religiosity, all his Christless morality and counted it as DUNG (see Philippians 3). This is true biblical repentance. Paul knew that before hearing God's Gospel and while being ignorant of the Righteousness of Christ Imputed (see Rom.10:1-4), he was a lost man. Not an ignorant, but nonetheless saved man, but a LOST man. The Bible states that if God's Gospel is hid, it is hid to them that are lost (2 Cor.4:3). Obviously then, before a man hears God's Gospel and believes and trusts in that Gospel, he is a lost man and not merely ignorant. What christendom has failed to do over the centuries is to actually define and distinguish the terms of God's Gospel from all counterfeits. Basically, 'christian' tradition has it that a man is saved if one believes in the existence of God and that His Son died on a cross for sins. This is NOT the Gospel, for if it was then most people would be saved. Many believe that they first get born again and then come to learn of God and what He has done for the sinner. But the Bible says otherwise. Scripture says that, "...faith cometh by hearing, and hearing by the word of God" (Rom.10:17). Ephesians 1:13 says that we trust Christ only AFTER we have heard this word of truth which is the Gospel of our salvation. Those who think that exactly what Christ did on the cross is just a theological sticking point among fellow 'believers', have got it drastically wrong. Who one believes Christ has died for reveals exactly what that person believes Jesus did on the cross. Far from being just a matter of high theology which can be debated amongst 'brethren', this is the core of Christianity itself. Who Christ is and what Christ has done is revealed in the Gospel by who Jesus died for on the cross. If one believes that Christ has died for every individual, then one holds to a salvation conditioned on the sinner's choice to accept or reject what has been done. If one holds to what the Bible teaches, that Christ died for His people, the elect of God, then one holds to the truth that what Christ did was actually obtain redemption for them by His death (Heb. 9:12). No matter how religious and moral a person is, NO ONE IS SAVED BEFORE THEY HEAR AND BELIEVE IN THE GOSPEL OF GOD. To believe that one was saved before hearing the Gospel, that is when the Gospel was hidden from them, is to base one's salvation on something other than God's Testimony. The Truth that is God's Gospel has yet to dawn on them. Those who place their faith in anything other than the obedience and death of Jesus Christ alone, have not God.

The doctrine of Christ is simply this: man is dead in sin (Eph.2:1,5), without God and without hope in this world (Eph.2:12). This means that there is nothing in man that can lead him to the true God. When asked who can be saved, the Lord Jesus replied "...with men this is impossible; but with God all things are possible" (Matt.19:26). This is in accord with the teaching just mentioned, that a man without God is without hope. Man has no hope of eternal salvation, of everlasting life without God. It is God Who makes alive, purely by His Sovereign grace: "But God, Who is rich in mercy, for His great love wherewith He loved us, even when we were dead in sins, hath quickened us together with Christ, (by grace ye are saved;)" (Eph.2:4,5; see also Col.2:13,14). "...of Him are ye in Christ Jesus..." (1Cor.1:30). God has chosen His people from among every nation to be His people, His very own elected children (Rev.5:9). God did this according to His Counsel: "Who hath saved us, and called us with an holy calling, not according to our works, but according to His own purpose and grace, which was given us in Christ Jesus before the world began" (2 Tim.1:9), and not, as many so falsely teach, according to His foreknowledge of who would choose Him. "In Whom also we have obtained an inheritance, being predestinated according to the purpose of Him Who worketh all things after the counsel of His own will"—not man's will (Eph.1:11).

    The Bible says that it is not because we love Him that God loves us, it is not we who have taken the initiative, but "we love Him because He first loved us" (1Jn.4:10,19; see also Rom.5:8). The Lord Jesus payed the penalty of all the sins of all the elect of God whom God had given Him (Isa.53:4,5) and has given them His

Righteousness: "Even as David also describeth the blessedness of the man, unto whom God imputeth righteousness without works" (Rom.4:6). God's Justice is satisfied for the penalty which God's elect had earned and has been met in full by Christ alone: "Christ hath redeemed us from the curse of the law, being made a curse for us: for it is written, cursed is everyone that hangeth on a tree" (Gal.3:13). We shall be presented to God faultless (Jude 24 & Col.1:22) for we are robed with Christ's perfect Righteousness: "I will greatly rejoice in the Lord, my soul shall be joyful in my God; for He hath clothed me with the garments of salvation, He hath covered me with the Robe of Righteousness..." (Isa.61:10). Jesus Christ alone has met the requirements of God's Holy law fully by His perfect obedience: "For as by one man's disobedience many were made sinners, so BY THE OBEDIENCE OF ONE shall many be made righteous" (Rom.5:19). All of God's elect will hear the Gospel and will, at the appointed time, believe it for this has been predetermined by God's immutable Counsel and Will (Acts 13:48). And, the Bible teaches that all for whom this has been done will never perish (Jn.10:27:28). They have been saved eternally and are preserved in Christ (Jude 1 & Psa.37:28). The life they now have is everlasting life which means that, not only will they live forever but they have, by the grace of God, been made alive unto Him eternally. None of God's children believe anything less, or more, than this simple Gospel as the only way to salvation. Christ said He is the Way to the Father (Jn.14:6). The way to God is not a life of good works, for the Bible says that by works shall no flesh be justified (Gal.2:16). A man is saved purely by God Himself choosing the man for salvation and by Christ's imputed Righteousness.

All who abide in the doctrine of Christ are preserved and their inheritance is reserved for them in heaven: "To an inheritance incorruptible, and undefiled, and that fadeth not away, reserved in heaven for you, who are kept by the power of God..." (1 Pet.1:4,5). All who reject the doctrine of Christ have not God and shall be eternally damned if they remain in that state: Whosoever transgresseth, and abideth not in the doctrine of Christ, hath not God. He that abideth in the doctrine of Christ, he hath both the Father and the Son. If there come any unto you and bring not this DOCTRINE, receive him not into your house, neither bid him God speed: For he that biddeth him God speed is partaker of his evil deeds" (2 Jn.9-11).

Please Contact:

morenodalbello@yahoo.com.au

Please Visit:

www.godsonlygospel.com

Made in the USA
Monee, IL
03 May 2026